Praise for
SOME OTHER WET LANDSCAPE

The woman is singing and talking to you and she is urgent. This "whittled woman/this battered blue fragment" has traveled far, has burst through harsh iterations of time and experience. In searing poems carried from the wreckages of marriage, of trauma-memory, of self-doubt toxic as glue, of once-sacred homes now vanished, McEniry's craft stays steady. Tough cadences and syllabic rigor thread themselves inside magic and enchanting music in a daughter's Sunday meal, a sea floor, a community of poets, and a "honey-mint whisper /of eucalyptus." There's more: wit and bite in the short lyrics a la Stevie Smith; and sound-bursts inside the spacious prose poems. Just when we're certain all is revealed of this wise and quirky soul-spirit-traveler, here comes young Eros, intoxicated by a lover's hair and a dove high in a tree where the poet declares: "I built the foundation of my summer/on her creation." This debut is a rare gift.

—Judith Vollmer, author of *The Apollonia Poems* (2017), winner of the Four Lakes Prize

Lynne McEniry's generous humanity and unswerving honesty shine in these poems of love and grief. Direct and down-to-earth in language and feeling, faithful to the sights and sounds of ordinary life, the poet meets herself through haunting encounters with others––on a street or plane, at a graveside, in a remembered bed or kitchen. Compassion and wry humor emerge, as well as the powerful sense that what has vanished is indelible.

—Joan Larkin, Lambda Award & Shelley Memorial Award winner, author of *Blue Hanuman* (2014)

some other wet landscape

poems

Lynne McEniry

Get Fresh Books, LLC
Union, New Jersey

Copyright © 2017 by Lynne McEniry

All rights reserved. No part of this book may be reproduced in any manner without written consent except for the quotation of short passages used inside of an article, criticism, or review.

Get Fresh Books, LLC
PO Box 901
Union, New Jersey 07083

www.getfreshbooksllc.com

Cover art & design: Raul Villarreal

Book layout: Leonardo Zuñiga

ISBN: 978-0-9989358-1-2

Library of Congress Control Number: 2017945506

Contents

My Son, Philip Seymour Hoffman, and Me..1

Real Day of the Dead..3

Things I've Not Yet Told You..4

At Poppy's 5 & 10..6

splinter..7

just like that..9

I miss Wallaby Farm..11

birdsong..12

ode to my scar: left eyebrow..13

An Occasional Poem for an Occasion for Which No One Asked Me to Write a Poem or Even Thought I Would or Should..14

If it's true what you write..15

it was..16

she comes to me in lilacs..17

Sunday Sauce..18

3J..19

Grand Theft, Lip Gloss..20

Locust Hill..21

I've always been afraid of astronauts..22

A Poem with Tray Tables in It...23

San Francisco Winds..25

spoon size Frosted Mini-Wheats..26

Locust Hill revisited: December 24, 2003.......................................27

blue, for Peter...28

No Woman, No Cry...29

ode to my scar: right kneecap...30

Olive Ridley...31

thin place..32

nesting...33

Ode to Tomato Soup...34

Once...35

morning hair..36

Poem for a Cousin Recently Dead..37

whittled woman...39

One Last Time..40

Confession...41

oral fixation..42

Bearing Out..43

mourning dove..44

Prince died..45

Later in life	47
good reasons to sweat to death	48
ode to my scar: right index finger	49
cutting a bagel as my father lay dying	50
Kemp's ridleys	51
Meeting Her Now	52
Dried-Up Things	54
first summer on Gerald Place	56
Places She Would Take Me	57
There on Locust Hill	58
Gramatan 5 & 10	59
Acknowledgments	61
Love and Gratitude in Abundance	62
About the Poet	65

for my parents, grandparents, great-grandparents ... in loving memory

>   Evelyn Veronica Fagan McEniry
>   David Joseph McEniry
>   Lillian (Billie) Agnes Regis Goldberg Gorton Fagan
>   John Kenneth Fagan, Sr.
>   Catherine Jones McEniry
>   William McEniry
>   Bridget Agnes McCarthy Goldberg Gorton
>   John Joseph Goldberg Gorton
>   and so on ...

Start children off on the way they should go, and even when they are old they will not turn from it.

—Proverbs 22:6

and may you in your innocence

sail through this to that

—Lucille Clifton

                                        Never mind.
                              The self is the least of it.
                              Let our scars fall in love.

                                        —Galway Kinnell

some other wet landscape

My Son, Philip Seymour Hoffman, and Me

I'm thinking about my son, and Philip Seymour Hoffman comes to mind. Does my son look like Philip Seymour Hoffman, or is it because I went to a Philip Seymour Hoffman interview and my son has a similar wit, similar wisdom, similar self-protectiveness to the five layers Philip Seymour Hoffman wore and then removed at least two of before the end of the interview? I'm thinking Philip Seymour Hoffman and my son would make good friends, and I recall Philip Seymour Hoffman saying he puts in earphones and jogs around the City in character, and inside my head it would be cool if he stopped for a bottle of water at the same place my son was waiting for a slice and they struck up a conversation and became friends. I think of *Pirate Radio* and how my son would probably love to be the Count, but should a mother want that craziness for her son? Then I'm thinking *The Savages* and how hard Jon Savage is trying to write and hold a relationship and help his depressed sister and their demented father when he says, *Death is gaseous and gruesome and it's filled with shit and piss and rotten stink!* and I think I'm like Philip Seymour Hoffman characters and wonder if I am like the real Philip Seymour Hoffman at all and how my son is like me and not and the ways I should have been better for him and his sister, and I think of *Doubt* when Father Flynn says, *Doubt can be a bond as powerful and sustaining as certainty. When you are lost, you are not alone,* and then I wish Phillip Seymour Hoffman had been Father Flynn on the stage because the play was so much better. I have imagined my son and myself strolling around BAM after a show saying, *Maybe we should head over to Junior's for a piece of devil's food cheesecake and a big thick mug of coffee,* and I'm telling my son Bill Murray is one of my favorite actors too and how he's got the lonely-guy-trying-to-make-the-best-of-it down pat but not clichéd and how, like Philip Seymour Hoffman, you know Bill Murray well, even as Todd DiLaMuca on *SNL,* and you know they are both good at their craft because you never feel like you are watching Philip Seymour Hoffman or Bill Murray unless you are actually watching them for their craft. I tell my son Bill Murray is a big supporter of Poets House and I wish I'd had the money to cross the bridge and eat dinner with him and Galway Kinnell last June because Galway Kinnell is one of my favorite poets and I wanted us to do that together, and he says, *Someday we will, Ma.* Someday. And I think of a *voice / spectral, calling you /* sister! */ from everything that dies,* and I say to my son, *Pal, please read again that copy I gave you of* The Book of Nightmares. And then he tells me that when he went to School of Visual Arts he met Bill Murray's son, or one of his friends was friends with him, and they went to a party at Bill Murray's house while he was away, but then he came home while they were all sleeping drunk on the floor, and Bill Murray was like, *Hey, what's all this,* and, *Come on, move along,* and all that kind of parent talk, but maybe just kind of tired and wanting his place to himself. While we look left, waiting for the light to change, Philip Seymour Hoffman is right there beside us and must think we look cool or sane or whatever, and he says, *Hey,* and my son says *Hey* back, and I stand with my mouth open, as usual, wanting to say something but feeling like whatever I would say would be the wrong thing, knowing that this will probably be just another missed opportunity. But my son, he says *Hey* right back with a nod, sticks out his hand, their eyes lock over the handshake, and my son says, *I admire your body of work,* takes his own hand back, puts it on my shoulder, guides me to the right, and we all move with the pedestrian flow.

Real Day of the Dead

Did you ever have sex on a bed topped with the coats of the mourners—friends and family downstairs eating three different casseroles, six kinds of pie, just hours after they buried their beloved below frozen December dirt? I should have known better than to ask, how she always turns the question back around on me, even knowing full well that I've taken only three lovers in the thirty-odd years since my first time, well two and a half, truthfully, since I couldn't bear to break the vow back in '89 ... bourbon and bowling and Bob, the ringer on Team Livin' on a Spare, made it mighty tempting ... 'til he moaned, *Right there, mamma*: his first gutterball of the night ... my first split ... and all these years later, on the real Day of the Dead, I find myself driving around town looking for a house full of mourners (the early dark and witch's moon make it easy to see inside), curtains pulled back on a family sitting Shiva, or there's a driveway full of neighbors carrying in covered dishes, and so I gather the nerve to go in, pretend I'm a work friend of the deceased as I scan the crowd for a lone mourner, ask him if I could walk him to the upstairs bedroom, help him find his North Face.

Things I've Not Yet Told You

I wanted to call you today, but I was sad. I wanted to say, *Hey you, I'm sad, and I don't want to talk about why … I just wonder if you wouldn't mind telling me about how the Kverneland plow is working, and hey, I keep meaning to ask you what "tedding the hay" means* … I want to ask you more things that we usually don't talk about, but that might lead back to what I was sad about before … before you started talking and making everything seem some kind of normal, so instead I think I might suggest we walk to our respective fridges and crack a beer together and talk something "all-American" on this holiday … not like how independence in this country doesn't mean independence for all … I mean like baseball, like you said you'd teach me, or if I have to take a turn talking, I can tell you everything I know about the maximum dump angle, lift capacity, and digging depth of a 1972 John Deere front end loader, just in case you ever gotta work one there. Or I'll ask you if you've got any good mechanical bull stories since I came across one for sale earlier today on Etsy, of all places, when I was debating whether or not to call you, and I got to wondering if you might have a bunch of mechanical bull stories, maybe mechanical bull stories from a bunch of different towns you passed through, or maybe just one awesome mechanical bull story that is the one to beat all mechanical bull stories worldwide … which got me to thinking about how me and you and Dennis and Laurie Ann would sit in the pub together twice each year, hanging out and being as silly as possible, avoiding the dark or sleep or poems or being alone or calling home, staying 'til everyone else was gone to bed, until the bartender, who said it made her happy to watch us being happy, said she had to lock up, though, before security came. But then I realized that we're all four in four different states now, and it's just not the same over Skype or FaceTime, but the four of us don't really use those things anyway … and the whole point is that I don't need to show anyone else the physical place I'm stuck in, which brings me right back to why I'm sad and why I want to call you but won't anyway. Or if I do, if the panic rests itself in my chest and starts my heart thumping to where I can hear it in my ears and I can't catch my breath sitting still and it's either call you from 296 miles and an ocean barrier away or bother my old neighbor Larry downstairs, pretending I heard another car thief out back while really just using him to make sure I'm not having a real heart attack or stroke or brain tumor this time. Anyway, it's the Fourth of July, and pretty soon fireworks will begin, and although I love them, the thing that makes me sad today has me housebound, and so I'll only listen to the booming, maybe see some pyrotechnic flashes creep in through the crack in the curtains, and I'll be thinking maybe this time next year, maybe I'll call you for real, not just think about it then, and ask you if the corn's knee-high and if you've been able to keep the poison ivy at bay, whether you've had time for windsurfing, and maybe I'll be able to tell you when you ask, *How ya doin', kiddo,* that I just had to call you because I just got up from lying on the earth and feeling my heart thumping as living colors exploded just for me, and Peter, I wasn't scared for a second that it might be a heart attack, because that pounding in my chest broke me wonderfully open to whatever rains down in the remnants.

At Poppy's 5 & 10

the world was ours.
If it was on the shelves
in the bins, even in the stock
room yet to be unpacked
we didn't have to ask.

Too young to work
the register, Poppy said my
job was to patrol the aisles, keep
an eye on things while he handled
business at the front counter. If I
needed backup I should ask.

Making my rounds, I saw
a woman in aisle three pocket
two bars of Irish Spring. I rushed
behind her, tugged her tattered
jacket sleeve, told her she should ask
Poppy first, but when her tired eyes
begged my consent, it was the first time
I understood there are other reasons
not to ask.

splinter

if I knew back then that one day I'd be
a grownup, that one day there might be
people who really just liked me for me,
for the sake of loving
someone because she is human and she craves
acceptance, desires love, and just wants
someone to care for her back, just maybe almost
as much as she cares for all of them, then maybe
I wouldn't have turned my head the other way
when Allie asked me to come play
at her house the first day off the junior high
bus, and maybe I would have taken a few minutes
to think about how she really just liked being
around me when she was the new kid
on the block just two years earlier   during those days
I was happy to swim in her pool and pretend
I liked Dawn dolls because it made her eyes
light up like eyes of joy I don't know if I'd ever
seen before on a child, because as she said we
were playmates, and she always wanted a
playmate, and I remember on the way out
her back door one day, her parents, who were
twice my parents' age, thanked me for being
so kind to their daughter because she didn't
draw many friends, and that day
I got off the junior high bus I forgot Allie's
kindness and her delight in me just because
I was me   and I turned my head when she called
after me, ran toward my first afternoon of
stolen cigarettes and beer warm
from being hidden in the bushes all night,
for a group of people who would never
care like Allie did about what book
I was reading or why I cried
myself to sleep most nights, and I continued
to turn my ear from her all through high school
when her eyes turned sad, and I knew I had some

part in that, but I needed more love, boy love,
dope love, love that helped me sleep at night
maybe even before the tears came, even when
I knew it was temporary love, love that led me
from home at 18, while Allie stayed on the block
in her parents' house with her sad eyes, no kids
ever coming or going, and when I had my own
kid not two years later, I came home and asked
my mother to watch mine so I could go knock
on Allie's door, so I could see if I could bring
the joy back, so I could ask if she still
had her Dawn dolls, if the pool was filled
for a swim, but then my mother got those
sad eyes, said, *Lynnie, I thought I told you
Allie died four months ago, and her parents
moved from the house the next day,* but I went
over there anyway and rubbed my hand up
and down the phone pole at the corner of
their yard until a big splinter punctured my
palm, and I left it there for four days, a day each
for Allie's eyes of joy and Allie's sad eyes,
and then I pulled it out, left the wound open

just like that

one minute she
was rambling on
apologetic about debts
incurred and time
misspent and her
instant mashed potatoes
were too heavy
to spoon into
her own mouth

next minute
she was planning
the annual picnic
remember she said
Auntie Mul's a
vegetarian now and
Tommy likes his
burger well done
with Swiss cheese

one sister packed
clothes the other
helped their mother
into bed for
her breathing treatment
one brother thought
life would be
easier once they
brought their mother
home tomorrow

the other brother
entered the room
as she lay
back for drugs
to take effect
like those potatoes

you didn't eat
he told her
with a grin
relief only takes
an instant

next morning
as they prepared
to meet the
undertaker with their
mother's favorite dress
the brothers and
sisters heard a
crash in the
kitchen and found
their father kneeling
in a heap
of glass shards
and fine grains
from a jar
of instant coffee

and to his
lips they saw
him holding her
last lipstick stained
brim

I miss Wallaby Farm

but not my ex who I used to go
there with during the first seven of our
28 years   I miss the cows lining up from
their stalls to process to the milking
machine, their path lined with manure
and gerbera daisies.

I miss how the machine made
the cows stand in a circle, the bovine version
of group therapy. And I miss imagining
them sharing their woes of knees
not made for getting back downstairs or the trials
of chewing for 16 hours a day with no top teeth.

I miss my wonder at engorged udders. I miss
whispering to the cows, *sometimes he's mean
to me when we're not here.* I miss asking
if they heard the one about the Pharaoh's dream,
whether they identified with the seven sleek cows
or the seven ugly cows, grass grazing or cow
cannibalism, seven years of bingeing
and purging or seven years of famine.

It's seven years now he's been my ex.
Before that, seven years of famine.
Before that, seven years of bingeing.
Before that, seven years of circles.
Before that, seven years of milking.

I heard that Wallaby sold out
to a development group
more than 20 years ago.

I miss wondering if the milking I witnessed
on the day I was there would become the
Wallaby's homemade mint chip ice cream
that I'd eat on our next visit.

I miss wrinkling my nose and grinning
at the same time: cow shit/gerbera daisies.

birdsong

*do you like to listen
to the birds?* I ask as we lie
in quiet morning light

I'm listening
to at least six different
birds, I think—warble, whistle,
and caw, a chatter,
a trill, and a tweet—
songs and calls that carry me

back to Mr. Weitz's seventh
grade "Listening to Today's
Music" class   my desk
on the third step up   my eyes
closed, ears attuned to the sound
of the sounds from the sound booth
where knobs and boards worked
together somehow to flood our
classroom with rock and acapella
reggae and rhythm and blues

Mr. Weitz played a game with us,
had us pick out all the instruments
we could hear in a song   he'd start
us out slow with acoustic
vs. electric in "Ramblin' Man," move
on to the brass in some Chicago
tune before dropping the tunes of
Orchestra Baobab, a melting pot
of sounds that carried me off to
a world outside the classroom walls

I like to listen too, you whisper as
the yellow-bellied sapsucker pecks
busily at some bark just outside
our window   I wonder how
I'd missed his sound earlier, wonder
where the birdsongs and calls
carried you in that quiet morning light

ode to my scar: left eyebrow

you are my
earliest, well-earned
in my first year of life—
baby's first steps meet
coffee table corner …
I only know
how you got here through stories
passed on about my father's obsessive
fears for his firstborn   each time
I pluck, you're here to remind me
    beware of pointed edges
what's the chance my father pulled
his hands back that day as I fell forward
knowing you'd be with me when
he no longer would

An Occasional Poem for an Occasion for Which No One Asked Me to Write a Poem or Even Thought I Would or Should

For Ysabel, a real-life Wonder Woman

Remember how we'd wait all day for the Enjoli commercial, thought we were so cool, smoking Kools in our mother's high heel shoes, carrying our father's briefcase full of blues. *I can bring home the bacon, fry it up in a pan, never let you forget you're a man.* Too young to work or cook or fuck, we knew we could do it, do that, do him, and do more if we could just get a spritz or two of that eight-hour perfume for the 24-hour woman. We didn't know any real life Enjoli women, but every time we enacted that 30-second spot we just knew that the good life would be ours if we could get our hands on that magic gold-bullet-shaped bottle. We'd be spritzing out gender slander in the name of power / love / money. For 30 seconds a few times each day we lived like Wonder Women. Every 30 seconds an occasion to fool ourselves into thinking we had it all when we had almost nothing at all. Little did we know that the singer of our favorite ditty was born a Norma, divorced a fourth time in her forties, and was the inspiration for a pink pig puppet. But never mind what's behind the scenes.

If it's true what you write
after "Belief System" by Roberto Carlos Garcia

Roberto, that we're only
remembered by how we make
love, then I'm afraid I'll be forgotten
before I'm dead, but I'm
hopeful that there's life after
50, and I wonder why
in this day and age that physical
love doesn't make sense to me
without some meaningful connection

I too believe in the magic
of kissing and dancing and
too much wine, but I also believe
they stop short of making us
make real love sometimes   I believe
in a love connection that defies
the physical while it craves the physical
is made shy by the physical and is
frightened by the physical and just
cannot go there for some damn reason
or another

I don't know
about everyone else, but when you
write like you do, Roberto, I love you
more, Roberto, and my language
touches your language, making mad
language love

it was

nothing

they said   the grinding engines
the trembling chandeliers

it was nothing to disturb
Lobster Extravaganza
on the first night of this funship voyage

it was
a ten-foot wooden rowboat
oar-less and bearing a hole

it was
ten men   skin burnt
close to being swallowed by the sea

gazing down from the eight decks
that separated
us   from   them
as the deckhands took each one aboard

I saw
ten men losing their grasp

the wet feet/dry feet policy
meant they must be sent
back to Cuba once we reached
dry land

I saw
ten men reaching
for me

she comes to me in lilacs

it isn't enough to inhale her
in the first spring bloom

or to search for her in each
significant bud

i find her under my naked feet
in sleepy winter roots

she whispers from under my naked feet

i have not abandoned you

Sunday Sauce

She helped line 11 cans under the opener and climbed up
to watch from the step stool while I set to work on the only

day with enough time. My daughter never tired as I hand-rolled
meatballs, pureed plump tomatoes, crushed garlic cloves, chopped basil

clipped from the sill garden, grated pungent Pecorino, Romano. At last,
all of it into her great-great-grandmother's pot, left for the day

to work its magic. No naptime for her on Sundays—of course
she wouldn't miss one chance to stir the simmering sauce.

The Irish make the best, she says when she invites me years later
to make the Sunday Sauce with her. It's a Friday night, and her grocery

doesn't stock our brand of tomatoes. In separate
small apartments now, we have no sill garden, no electric opener,

yet we set to work in her kitchen—she lines and grates and hand-rolls,
I puree and crush and chop, and we brown and blend together

in Gigi's cast-iron pot. We order some takeout, pop in an old movie,
and before it ends we are aware of a hint of a familiar, fresh aroma.
It still works,

Tara shouts, pulling me behind her to the stove. She tears two chunks
of crusty bread from a loaf. As I lift the lid the scent embraces us—

heady, savory sweet. We sink our bread down into the pot and soak
up Sunday Sauce on Friday night. Immersed in its heat we laugh as it

drips from elbows, from chins, down the sides of our cast-iron pot.

3J

exiting the Saw Mill River
Parkway I am 12
years old again

instinct directs me to turn
right onto Valley Road
where the Sabrett man waits
for factory workers on lunch breaks

in the driver's seat
I push my slight self forward
hold my breath   rock back
and forth to help the engine make
the great incline

DeHaven Drive is just
around the corner now
and I know that Poppy will have
saved his extra parking spot for us

I race for the door so I can
be the one to work the intercom
that will signal Nonna to buzz us in

Grand Theft, Lip Gloss

Seventh grade, we were so
cool, going to the high school
football game and then Candy
peer pressuring us to sneak past
the crowds heading for shitty
refreshments, to run down
the dirt path and across the big two-lane
highway to Two Guys. I knew Candy
liked to take things that didn't belong
to her, so while we were in Cosmetics
looking at lip gloss, I got to thinking
of Poppy complaining about
the price of theft insurance, eating
the loss when it happened at his five and dime.

Two steps out the door, a man
grabbed us each by the arm, took us
to a back office, made us empty
our pockets, said we were lawbreakers
now, and our photos would be sent to store
managers up and down Route 46. I recall
the shiny glass bottle, its sleek roller ball,
the sweet smell of strawberries when I opened
the Lip Smackers cap at the counter that day.
But I'm fuzzy on the details, if Candy
slipped it into my pocket that day or if I
lived up to her dare.

When people ask, *Have you ever shoplifted?*
I don't lie. What I've carried inside me
all these years is whether I was more ashamed
I'd wet myself on my walk home that day, or
how I appeared to my parents once I got there …
Desire and piss is what I recall
when a shop clerk asks, *May I help you?*

Locust Hill

On the day the stone is set
we pilgrimage

to my mother's grave
her husband   children   grandchildren

and since tomorrow
would be her birthday someone suggests

balloons
tied to bright colored strings   another suggests

flowers
a miniature red rosebush   we arrive

empty-handed   we read
August 17, 1945–June 3, 1997

our grief is raw   private
even among each other   so we stand

at her feet   each approaching
the stone alone   my father spit-shines

her name with his handkerchief
her grandson sets down

his Walkman and presses play
headphones plugged in so only his Nonna can hear

when it's my turn I step too close and
dirt sinks under the weight of sorrow

I am being
sucked into the underworld

relieved my mother
wants me with her

I've always been afraid of astronauts

is a thought that shoots quick like a sailfish
across my mind   even though their outfits
and their apparatuses are quite similar to deep
sea divers and I've no fear of them, I think,
as I sit in the cool sand on a warm summer night
and you there with me   watching stars
over the sea   you there singing a tune
about romping around cosmic galaxies
pointing out Pisces and Cancer in the New
England sky   telling me how we don't need
a net to reel them in   so I try to entice you
with the thrill of the catch or the delight
in the bright colors of crab and clown fish
I want to shed my fear with these flippers
and goggles   believe that we'll be as safe
with the gamma rays as we are with
the stingrays   that you'll teach me
to wait out the blinding dark nebula and share
in its revelation

A Poem with Tray Tables in It

The guy next to me on the flight was a nervous wreck ... shaking both knees nonstop, taking the inflight magazine out, then putting it back in, then taking it out again ... The window shade went up then down. I wanted to see the Rockies, it was my first trip ever to the West Coast, wanted to watch the landscape change, but he wouldn't let me, plus it was like he couldn't get far enough away from me in his seat. I didn't want to take out my breakfast, knew my size was disgusting him, making him nervous, the way he'd glance, the way he watched me struggle to buckle the seat belt, hogged the whole armrest even as he turned his shoulder inward, pointed both knees toward the window, didn't even want his sneaker touching mine, like the fat would rub off on him. I wanted to put the tray table down, get my notebook out, write a poem just like this one, but I didn't want him to see my words, didn't want to hurt his feelings, didn't want to shame him like he was shaming me ... It was too small a space, and besides, I was afraid that the size of my stomach wouldn't let the tray table rest flat on my lap ... And it was too small a space there in row 34, seats B and C ... too small and not enough oxygen to bear my shame and his. And so instead of lowering my tray table, I put my hands in my lap and turned my mind away from the tray table in front of me to the tray tables we had when I was a kid ... the metal kind ... white trays rimmed in gold, each with a Monet fruit still life, tray tables with thin brass legs that fold neatly flat and hang on a stand for storage ... And when the tray tables came out from back deep of the hall closet, we knew something special was going on ... company? Banquet fried chicken in front of the TV? Maybe a rare family game night? I thought of how lucky we were—we didn't have much, but the tray tables were an extravagance, something especially special. And I remembered how we would take the tray tables with us to visit family on the holidays ... our something special to add to the celebration when we had no money for store-bought cake or a bottle of wine. I remember how sad I was the day after Christmas when my mother had been too tired to put the tray tables back into the back of the closet and one became the latest victim during my brothers' hell-raising. The metal leg snapped clean in half. And right there on that airplane in row 34, seat B, I mourned that tray table and the fact that we were then down to three every time company came, and on Banquet fried chicken nights, so some of us would have to share, or maybe Mom wouldn't even let us get them out since there were four of us kids and only three tray tables. And after the plane landed and we were taxiing to our gate, 34 C now opened the window so I could see a runway that looked like every other runway. And I began to think about my destination and if I'd see Mount Rainier from the highway, so I reached under the seat for my bag, and while my head was down I guess 34 C thought if he couldn't see my ears then I couldn't hear him saying into his phone, *I'll be off the plane in five minutes unless this fat bitch does a slow sidestep down the aisle*. Until everyone in the 33 rows ahead of us got off the plane, I sat in my seat with my tray table down.

San Francisco Winds

your honey-mint whisper
of eucalyptus leads me
to your mighty hush
among the redwood,
your Stinson sea-sprayed
secrets are safe with me,
oh beach where calla lilies
grow like New Jersey dandelions,
their slender bodies upturned
wedding dresses   dancing
and dipping with each gust.
oh San Francisco winds …
oh murmurs of Marin, oh winds
soaring deep and
tumbling up, and then over
to your Beat brothers' raspy
gin-soaked squalls
reverberating in the
Vesuvio / City Lights alley,
oh City by the Bay,
your screeching street
and clanging cable cars—
winds of promise,
winds of peace,
hippy dippy winds of Haight,
and the sassy, ballsy breeze
blowing any which way
up and down the Castro
while the sibilant winds of
past and present sinners
and saints find sanctuary
at Mission Dolores and Alcatraz.
oh Fog City winds
gusting around the trusses
of your only Golden Gate,
release me.

spoon size Frosted Mini-Wheats

it poured rain today, a rain I prayed might be falling right now in San Francisco too, all over the whole of dehydrated California, please God, so I didn't mind the rain one bit until I had to walk back and forth across campus twice before noon, my clothes then soaked through on my body through three mock interviews, a tutor with a migraine, and consultants telling us the hard work is just about to begin when we thought we'd been in the thick of it for the last three years, and I didn't get home until after seven and the zucchini had gone to mush, which was to be my main meal because I'm trying to eat double the vegetables and low carbs, and so I eat the chicken breast cold and alone and then turn to pet my dog, looking to her for some of that unconditional love, and I feel a tick on her chin so, too late for the vet and my body itching all over with thoughts of it crawling out of her and onto me in the night, I get some tweezers and rubbing alcohol, but she's no fool and lifts her lip and snarls mean at me like never before, this fluffy adorable dog I've nicknamed Shorty Long and Biggie Smalls and Doxie Doodle, as if her real names, Aquinna Dench McWinters, or Quinnie, or Quinn Quinn, or Denchie, as Jude likes to call her, aren't cute enough, and for the very first time she doubts my motives, mistrusts the hand that pets her, and this dog, she won't stop barking for hours after all that snarling, won't even take a Milk-Bone from me or a piece of cheese, the good stuff from the aged section at Gary's, when suddenly I'm in a heap on the hardwood, adding my own howling to Quinnie's, and I find myself moaning repetitively, *I want my mom*, and I wish I could go to her house right now, where there'd be pot roast warming on the stove top or my top three favorite cereals with a whole gallon of whole milk, ice cold, waiting for me, and I'd forget how invisible and useless I felt at work earlier today or how my dog's need for comfort had to come before my own or how when I was little I daydreamed daily about breaking a leg and needing a full-length cast or some such illness or injury so that all that attention I never received being the oldest of four in a row would be showered on me at this moment right here on the hardwood, even though my parents are buried long and deep and I've a milk sensitivity, and even though Quinnie has buried her tick-infested head in the crook of my neck and has settled herself to lapping up tears while I imagine her tongue a magical rain cloud big as the whole Golden State

Locust Hill revisited: December 24, 2003

Rien à faire.
                    —*Beckett*

nothing
could have warned us of the weather
we had rock salt and shovels
at the door for days before   waiting for death for snow
children and grandchildren woke
together in his house   it had been raining
all night   if it were cold enough
for snow we'd be measuring it in feet
it was up to us
to console the mourners   *we understand—*
get back on the road to your last-
minute shopping and wrapping   we will
be fine   at the cemetery   on our own
the groundskeeper
told us we could not bury our father
that day—the hole they dug
kept closing in on itself   umbrellas
and boots useless as we slogged
to the chapel for final farewells

we told the piper of course he should go
but he soldiered on   an extra
raincoat over his pipes as he
played us out of our cars and back again

blue, for Peter

The blue of your T-shirt made me

a wave   vastness from nowhere, seven
or eight feet before the curl, great swell
as far as Jersey waves go, a fine line sprayed
off itself, but Jersey waves aren't true blue
any way you look at them.

Your worn cornflower shirt

and I want clear sky   a dome's
worth to get the grades, all shades
from the pale almost-white horizon blue
to the gray-blue squint of my eye, the robin's
shell, or the room that awaits a brand-new boy.
Some azure, some baby, some powder, your shirt
cradles you all curly and loose and bluesy.

I saw your blue and hummed

some blue songs   "Famous Blue Raincoat"
came to mind, the parts I could remember,
then "Blue Moon" to "Blue Monday," "Blue
Velvet," and "Blue Suede Shoes." But once
you let Dylan in it's hard to send him
away, so I spent that day into night
all "Tangled Up in (your) Blue."

No Woman, No Cry

I'm eating breakfast on a dune,
sun over my left shoulder, languid
low tide waves waving,

and Bob Marley, Sunday morning guru.
Usually I skip breakfast, but today
I take a chance on the dollop of what looks like

Gulden's Spicy Brown
alongside my French toast. *Everything
all right?* the waitress asks as I linger

over my third coffee, the sun rising, and cinnamon
sugar butter. I could swear she added
little sister to her concern,

reminding me of the good people
I have lost
too quick, too deep.

ode to my scar: right kneecap

I just wanted to be cool, and I really
thought I was for about 10 minutes,
tooling around the block a few times
on my new blue Schwinn with Sue
on the handlebars, my bare feet grasping
rubber pedals as we laughed out loud
with the wind   my loose T-shirt caught
a breeze, just enough to expose the bottom
of my finally blooming breasts, and I
praised God for good timing on both
accounts as I rounded the corner and
smiled wide seeing *him* there to witness
my epiphany   in the same instant
that I drew up the courage to catch
his eyes, I saw him ogling Sue, her
long brown hair blowing back
in my face   and I knew then why
she asked for the ride in the first place
and why he happened to be there
on the corner just then   as I reached
to yank down my T-shirt I swerved
and hit the curb   and just like in every
ABC After School Special, he saved
Sue as I skid alone on the asphalt
as the doctor extracted seven pebbles
from my knee, I was glad for a reason
to weep

Olive Ridley

Some unpredictable act
calls this olive ridley back

to the sands of her conception.
She paddles ashore to do her work

among the ancient aggregate.
Swollen, she swims toward the arribada,

ensuring the odds for a few of the hundreds
she will deposit in her nest.

At nightfall she digs
with the weight

of what she carries, tossing aside
grains until she has created the warm teardrop

essential for incubation.
This olive ridley

forgives her trespassers and drags
herself back into the sea, trusting

that some will crawl
to the surface.

thin place
after Jean Valentine

leave fear
on your pillow she says
when we meet in this
thin place   no fear
in this thin place
she says without
moving her lips   my hand
reaches easily inside
to remove my fear knot   no mess
just release as I follow her eyes
place fear on the ocean floor   just
inside the coral door to this   thin place
where we've met again   she reaches
for my hand   buoys me
as I float   from dark dream to daylight

nesting

driving along   windows down
the first spring day
she makes 72 strokes
through her long brown hair   gathers
what remains and releases
strands into warm breeze

cavity   cup   pendulum
the most common nests
understory   midstory   canopy
the places birds build nests
she tells me and I think
let them incubate their eggs
in my love's hair

birds will build nests
with the hair of the one I love

we go on like that for miles
me driving   she brushing
and releasing her hair

Ode to Tomato Soup
after Galway Kinnell

Home late from the reading, I haven't
tasted a drop of the velvety soup filling
the cream-colored bowl before me. Still
trying to live with the news of your
passing today, I realize now I'll never
eat another bowl of creamy tomato again—
the color of hell's flame, heaven's
blazing heart, the color of the poet's apple
brandy lipstick keeping me captive earlier
tonight as she read the words of another poet
while we're all dying a little inside knowing
you would never again let another poem loose
into this nightmarish world.

I never did like oatmeal, Mr. Kinnell, although
that poem of yours made me smile inside—
"Oi 'ad a 'eck of a toime" each time I read it,
time traveling with you and Keats schooling
me on craft and image, and you were in autumn then
as we are in autumn now, the last for you, an ironic
time for a poet to go. I take my bowl to the sink,
dump the soup down—a bloodletting. I take out
a package of Quaker Instant, apples and cinnamon,
just right for this autumnal feast that I will
maybe eat—alone.

Once

to win the heart of a boy I listened to him talk about
crankshafts and camshafts and driveshafts and overdrive,
and when listening wasn't enough I learned the difference
between boxed and open, fixed and adjustable, Allen
and ratchet, so I could hand them to him when he was under
the hood, learned even quicker the obvious fact that
babe, there's a fucking world of difference between 1/4 and 3/8,
which might have been my first clue, but I was deep
in love with the confidence and wisdom that a '69

Rally Sport, a hardcover *Chilton's Repair Manual*, and a full-
time job in the family business give a guy. I even convinced
myself that knowing how to change a radiator, change
brakes, change spark plugs, change fan belts and timing
belts and drive belts would serve me better in the long run
than going from high school to Katherine Gibbs Secretarial
School when my parents couldn't pay Federal Mortgage Corp.
or JCP&L or NJ Bell or even school hot lunches for three kids
younger than me. And so I took all the tips I made at R Gang

Sandwich Shop that month and bought an AutoMeter Street Rod
Designer Black Tachometer, the most expensive single
item I ever purchased. And the night he mounted
it on his dash, wired it to his engine, and the gauge proved
how high performance his car was, he took me to Arby's
to celebrate. It was there that he told me we were made
for each other, we made a good team, pulled out a box
from Kay Jewelers and proposed marriage. When I left

him 26 years later, I walked past a Harley Sportster
motor on our dining room table on my way to phone a friend
for a ride because all three vehicles in the driveway had his
name on their pink slips. I still don't own my own car, still
deal with the shame of asking for rides. While I have pumped
some gas, refilled some wiper fluid, and once filled four
tires with air, I'm happy I could choose to break off
my intimate relationship with what's under a hood. Sometimes
when I'm a passenger and I feel a drag on acceleration
or a grinding at stop signs, I find myself frustrated, thinking about
what parts we'd need to fix it right.

morning hair
Torii Kotondo, color woodblock print

brushing bangs from my eyes I feel
for myself,
find a stray clip, a knotted clump, a thread
from his blue battered necktie

in the mirror I see the remains
of last night's careful
coif created in hope of a lover's
swoon, styled to take his attention upward,
bearing the weight of first impressions

I wish he saw my early
morning hair   stray wisps sneaking
out, seeking attention from my cheek, still dreaming

confused
about their place on my scalp, yet
   searching,

reaching,
      wandering
just the same

my morning hair thinks
for itself   goes
where it wishes

Poem for a Cousin Recently Dead

How for all those seven years, all the generations before me were dying, 10 of them in seven years— mother, grandfather, grandmother, grandmother, father, a few aunts and uncles

in between, and two in-laws of my generation dead, one just three weeks after my father's death, but I was barely treading water then—an orphan at 40, the oldest woman left in the bloodline.

So when I learned last week that a cousin died, exactly one year older than me, the first of our generation to die, my first thought was *thank God for his twin so I'm not the oldest*

of our generation too. The next thought was fear for my own heart, trying to keep pumping in this fat body, my lungs working hard core overtime, particularly on stairs and steep inclines.

Am I next? Is that spring dream I had in which I faced a neon sign blinking, "DEAD AT 54" (next August, by the way), an omen?

Although I've been working hard at this meditation bit, I can't kick the mantra that comes to me without prompting a few times each day: *God, please help me; I don't want to die,*

which multiplies the fact I can't quit fear-eating a pint of Phish Food and a bag of Wavy Lays each night. After dark. Alone. And who the hell am I to make this cousin's death about me

anyway? I should be adopting a new mantra ... *God is the love in which I forgive you, Cousin ... God is the love in which I forgive myself ... God is the love in which I forgive you, Cousin ... God is the love in which I forgive myself ... God is the love in which I forgive you, Cousin ...*

You, Cousin, abused as a child, then turning that powerlessness into abuse against my sister and me while you charmed my friends while I watched in silence ... you,

Cousin, living cross-country for the last 25 years to escape the law … you, Cousin, who "died of alcohol," as the cop said when reporting your passing. I don't want to die of food.

And I think of the rest of my blood generation—our laundry list of self-help remedies, anxieties, addictions … what is it with our bloodline, and what have I set up for my own kids, now grown,

my platelets and plasma floundering around in their vulnerable veins? And can we all kick this together, maybe propose a new reality show to the networks, some combination of *Addicted*

and *The Biggest Loser—Survivor: Multigenerational Edition? God is the love in which I forgive you, Cousin; God is the love in which I forgive myself. God is the love in which I forgive*

whittled woman

it began as a fragment
of an old medicine bottle
deep blue and
dirty,
tossed overboard
by a sailor with stomach trouble

    *

walking the shoreline
she knew the Sea Glass
Association collectors hunted
reds, blacks,
coveted oranges
to fill trays and fashion trinkets,

but she treasured abundant
greens and blues most of all

    *

those perigean tides come around only twice each year

what were the odds
this whittled woman,
this battered blue fragment,
would arrive on the same shore, same time
after the century's turn, a new war raging

One Last Time

Nine years since the divorce, since we
laid our heads on the same pillow and talked
quietly in the night about how many eggs
were in the fridge or whether my mother actually
smiled at us before her last breath. Nine years
since we hurt each other, since everything
we thought we knew about each other
circled about us in the early morning air
around our bedroom window, became those particles
we see swirling in a beam of sunlight
but can't gather up in our arms to try
to make whole again, nor can we send them off
out the window with a swish of the arm. Nine years
since we've had any conversation at all, and all
this time I've been fine with that … too much
hurt had happened in our 28 years to make even
pleasantries possible at our daughter's wedding just
two years ago. And yet tonight, my head alone
on my pillow at 4 a.m., as our kids wipe the sleep and some
tears from their eyes and head out from their homes
to meet in Newark to fly nine states away to meet
you to say a final farewell to your mother as she
breathes her last breaths, is the first time
in nine years I wish I could be there too   wish I could
arrive with the kids and remind you
of how good and kind you were with my mom
in her last days and how very sorry I am it's your
mom now and to help you remind your dad
that he has us and the kids, the way we reminded
my dad of exactly that   and how very sorry I am
that I forgot to buy eggs nine years ago   to make
you a civilized breakfast at least that one last time

Confession
for Yesenia

Neither do I know
how to love
properly

My hands, though, are more
palms shut, palm holding too
tight to palm, making sweaty

palms, palms fooling
themselves, palms pressed too tight,
one unto the other, until my heart

line and my life line are too
blurred for the most practiced
of palm readers, and I'm left with nothing

to show for it and stand mumbling
my historical stories of my lack, my longing

        If only love   then safety
                          then release

but not really release trapped there
like garden dirt packed tight under
each nail, like the microscopic bumps

of the five-year-old
wart, the blue veins bulging
when fingers squeeze tight,

when palms and fingers strangle
for fear of letting
go

oral fixation

there once was a little girl who spoke
to herself in whispers for fear
that asking for a hug would go unheard
by parents too drunk too poor too tired from four
kids under five needing on them
all the damn time,
who grew to be a girl who cracked
her gum in silent defiance right in front
of the math teacher who shouted
WRONG at her weekly for the whole
class to hear, who grew into the girl who learned
to hold a bong hit the longest to make up
for trying to talk about books
outside the classroom,
who grew into the girlfriend who talked
cars *like a guy*, who grew into the young wife who gave
a good blow job in trade for some
conversation, who grew into the mother *who swallow(ed)
that cum if you don't want another kid yet*, who grew
into the woman who chain-smoked and kept
her thoughts to herself, who chewed ice cubes
for comfort, who grinded her teeth to keep
the words in, who stopped wearing lipstick
so as not to call abusive attention to the fact
she even had a mouth, who chewed the inside
of her cheek to silence the rage, who grew fat
by opening her mouth only for artificial
sweetness, only when nothing else
seemed to work,
who grew into a woman so large
she actually became
invisible

Bearing Out

It took eight years
and an Under Construction
sign on Yonkers Raceway
for the shock
to wear thin enough

Why change the track?
Facing it in Central Ave.
traffic I cried

for horses and jockeys
making rounds somewhere else,
cried for days past when I would pick
Abracadabra to win
and you would place
the dollar bet for me,

Johnny Carson for company
while I waited for you
with Lorna Doones and milk

until after midnight, and you'd come home
to tell me you doubled
my money or to wish me
better luck next time
that pounding hooves meet dirt

They demolished the grandstand
in the three numb months
between your death and hers,

my mother, your daughter
At fifty-one, she died

Wasn't that enough?

You were old, though
You were supposed to die

mourning dove

for weeks I watched a mourning
dove carry twigs and butts and strands
of long brown hair up to the insides
of the flowering plum growing 37 years
since you bought the place   as blossoms
withered before red leaves would grow
I could see from my perch on the deck
the home that dove fashioned from odds
and ends she salvaged from around our
yard   I built the foundation of my summer
on her creation—magic trick of nature:
such a small, soft being building something
indestructible from random discarded scraps

Prince died

and Doris Roberts died, and Monica at work, her mother died too,
and there were two Sisters from the convent who died ... The
dying has been busy,

and all we need to do is turn on the news or wait in line at the grocery store to hear of another dead person, another person waiting to die,

and I am so scared to die, so death obsessed it's like I just keep
sedentary on purpose so I can say to myself *I told you so*

when I drop dead of a heart attack or find myself in the ER
with white coats all around telling someone I love about the newest

procedure ... Will I need stents or stints or shunts, and what is the
difference, or are those even real things? And today I sit here with a
pain running

from the core of my left breast, just off to the right of the nipple
is where it originates, then down my left arm, where it throbs a bit
mid-upper-arm before

traveling down to the wrist, a trail of radiating pain that ends in
some slight finger numbing. There's also some pulsation on the left
side of my neck, and let's not

forget the weary, weary spine ... All of this is to say I've felt it all
before   or else, wait—this isn't exactly the same way I've felt it
before, and how many times ...

It's only my body is so weak from the weight it carries because I
force it to bend and twist and walk and sit in ways I have no right
to expect it

to perform after all the abuses I inflict. And I'm scared because my
mom died at 51, and my dad died at 63, and I am nearing 54, and
when will people be saying

it was me? And I want to live, sweet Jesus, I want to live healthy as hell until just before death at 86, as three of my grandparents did, so I want to get

better, and I know how to do it, but every day I try again, every single day I do, oh God, but then food and that inner voice from an 80s game show …

I wanna press my luck even though I really don't, but it's like the only fucking risk I take, and it's like Prince singing "Face Down," and it's like

Doris Roberts being Ray Romano's fat annoying mother who no one listens to, because it's always the same old story, like the boy who cried wolf and I

would rather be the wolf, but I don't know how to be, and I think that's why the wolf is my spirit animal (that or the sturgeon, depending on which website)—

not because I am like the wolf but because I must learn from the wolf, so Wolf Spirit and God in heaven and Prince and Doris and Philip Seymour Hoffman and Pete Seeger and Galway Kinnell,

I don't want to die tonight. I want to be home in my favorite old sweatshirt surrounded by good books and good music and bad television and the will to help me save myself.

Later in life

I retired from poetry and set to growing and selling beefsteak tomatoes in front of my seaside shack from a crate I made out of scraps from my driftwood collection with my dead father's hammer and level, and since I had also made a money box and trusted the honor system like I was taught at CSE, I had more time on my hands and turned to writing memoir, but after a few months or a few chapters—whichever came first—I realized I was writing a prose poem, so I bought some new Bics, dug out my Drew hoodie from beneath the moth balls, dusted off my journal, turned to where I had left off mid-sentence and reentered the workforce on commission.   And then later in life when the soil all around my shack was oil-destroyed forever, I retired from poetry because I had to take on a third job because social security dried up and health insurance was abolished and the cap on raising the rent broke through the ceiling at 30 percent each year. No such thing as food stamps, no gas for Meals on Wheels, and you had to be under 18 or over 80 to even stand in the bread line, and so I was wandering the streets alone, wearing only insecurity under my moth-eaten coat of shame.   And so later in life, when I retired from poetry, it didn't take long for dementia to set in, and my mind ate my mind with nothing else to do—no meditations in an emergency—and it really was hard to master the art of losing a common language, and I was living in the book of nightmares, the terrible stories.   But then later in life, when I had been retired from poetry and my mind was slowly still eating its way through itself, the Crew intervened and wrote down the dates of residency readings and Roman's retreats on my calendar in fat red Sharpies, and Mary devised a schedule of who would pick me up when … Some things never change … They labeled my pantry shelves, and the Crew filled them to overflowing: haikus and elegies and odes and ghazals and bops and sonnets and ballads and narratives and lyrics and then stocked my medicine chest with metaphor, enjambed lines   white space   tercets, meter, and a healthy dose of ambiguity. They hung photos of Joan and Alicia and Anne Marie and Jude, Jean and Laura too, so I could remember who taught me in the first place, and when all their hard work was done, someone chose a dance party mix, dropped their iPhone in a coffee mug, and we were up all night to get lucky.

good reasons to sweat to death
after Darla

because you laden your camel with at least twice the amount of water you'll need to make your trek across the Sahara Desert but end up giving it all away to a family of four, stranded in their jeep and dangerously dehydrated because they used the last of their water to feed the radiator with the hope of completing their pilgrimage to honor their roots

because after a lifetime of swimming just off shore with whales, you change it up and attempt to outswim the pyroclastic flow of Kilauea

because Johnny Depp and Hunter Thompson are now the *Sweatin' to the Oldies* instructors

because of an honest day's work on a chain gang breaking up asphalt and carrying large portions of it out to a cleared field in the sun near the Texas/Mexico border, where you are a member of Team Freedom, who has been planning for months the escape of one of your cellblock mates—a guy who crossed over from Mexico to work his ass off to earn money for a lifesaving operation for his child and who was placed on death row because he looked *exactly* like one of the three white guys who robbed the Rio Grande National Bank

because your Crew writes like they are on fire and you can't help gathering their stanzas in your arms, rolling nude in their images, French kissing their metaphors, and then swallowing them whole to feed your core's hungry furnace

because you're an astronaut who made it from planet Earth into the heart of the Red Spider Nebula

because Sosha has sweet-talked you into climbing into the beautifully tiled brick oven to eat a pizza at the exact moment of perfect doneness

because you've gone to Death Valley to live out the literal paradox of being at the lowest of lowest places below sea level and the highest of high temperatures at the very same time

because I'm your Venus   I'm your fire   your desire

ode to my scar: right index finger

I wince and feel my stomach
turn each time I rub another
finger over the thread-thin
line right where the tip
of the finger bends   and I recall
how you came to be—
bored teenager, hot summer day,
and a few cans of Schaeffer snuck
from the fridge   a dare I couldn't
tear the can in half   it felt so
thin   I bent it back and forth
a few times   lid to bottom
lid to bottom until I got two
good cracks in the tin   until I could
see the silver insides   a golden
sip or two left if I wanted   and then I heard
my mom calling me home from
the other side of the block   and with
the rush of the fear that she'd caught me
the can ripped in two with an accidental
last twist   leaving me with six thin
stitches and a scar so I'd never forget   what?
spending high school mornings drinking
my father's beer, or not realizing
skin is so thin—

cutting a bagel as my father lay dying

turn the blade away from yourself
was his fierce final warning
you can hardly anticipate
edge severing edge
six layers
deep

Kemp's ridleys

Kemp's ridleys close by, braving
New England waters   and early
in the season too   with my dream
eyes I see you swimming
in the deep right here, with right
whales and jellies   although frigid
you flock to these chockful
feeding grounds   neither of us
has time enough to wonder—
does courage or cowardice lead
more quickly toward extinction?

Meeting Her Now

> *we tilt toward each other,*
> *the ground is softer*
> *than I thought,*
> *our foreheads touch.*
>   —*"The Changing Coat,"* Anne Marie Macari

How I couldn't decide if she was adorable or horrible, but I knew for sure I envied her forehead, unfurrowed and kissable, the photo showing your forehead resting on hers, and Anne Marie's poem comes quick to my mind mixed with my mixed emotions about meeting her this way, that this first time meeting her would well likely be the last time, and why did you wait for this time, and did you always mean to wait for now, or did shit just get in the way? All my imaginings about her before were about something like whether people were kind to her when she was young and the ways she was kind to you, and could she love you enough to let you be alone when you needed that and to stay deep in your pocket when you needed that too, but meeting her now I feel somewhat betrayed by her playful smile, the gleam in her eye, and surely now my curiosity about her is more about my curiosity about you, and so I move from her forehead away from her, down angle and curve of your profile from the shadow of your right eyebrow to where your throat meets your chest, the muscles and tendons extending from deltoid to clavicle, and I want to rest my head on your soft shoulder, but I travel up from your neck to your hairline that makes me think I want to pet those alpacas you taught me about the first time we met and down to the string around your neck, holding the token I know pretty well but cannot see there, and I pause there for a moment to wonder if the string and the token are a connection to her, and if so, have you loosened the string, or are you wearing the token down, rubbing it between left forefinger and thumb as you write or you drive or you fight to fall asleep? And the angle of the photo makes the water and the boat and the hill in the background dip sharply from left to right, and I try to imagine the cut of your hair and the length of your beard when I saw you just two months ago, as I tilt my own head down to the right, wondering where in the water you are and whether she loved you most of all when she shot this or if she was playing for the camera, and is this your favorite one or one of the last ones of you together, and what season is it, and where exactly is that hill in the distance, and why did you choose for me to meet her this way at this time? And do you think we would have liked each other? You're tanner than she is, and you're in a boat together. Or are you? And are your eyes really gleaming? Is your hand holding hers? What are you each thinking the second the image is captured? And you, I pray you won't be long lonely, not meaning there has to be another love in another photo for you not to be lonely. Oh, you know what I mean, and you get my clumsiness with words—and my awkwardness around meeting new people—and I try to make sense of the picture without her in it, this new person I just met tonight for the first time and last time, and I wonder if I'll meet your next love this same way.

Dried-Up Things

Millena remembered when sexy Miranda's son's fell off
and the cat caught it midair before it hit the nursery carpet.
Christine keeps her daughter's in a ziplock baggie
so they can admire it right there in plain view.
Amanda's is secured in a film canister, and her mother shares
their indigenous tale of connection every time they take it out to
remember. Alex said she was all grossed out when she had to pick
up her little brother's and throw it in the trash can.
Lauren shared the passage they read in *Dwellings* where Linda Hogan
made an umbilical bag to contain that first point of connection.

The rest of the class listened in varying degrees
of shock and awe. Who would have thought
our *Lunch Poems* conversation would turn
toward this ... that Frank's "Rhapsody" and "The Day
Lady Died" would bring to us the music of the city
and Billie Holliday, who shared today's date
as her birthday with my son, also born
April 7th, 33 years ago today. And just after
I wished Wayne a happy day first thing
this morning, my brother called to say an estranged
cousin—just about the same age
as my son—was laid out, as we spoke,
at Duchynski-Cherko and not at Flynn's
or Sinatra's, where the rest
of the Yonkers family's bodies were last seen. And did I
mention that Billie Holiday was born a Fagan,
just like my mother was ... and her father ... and that
my mother's father married a Billie ... and that
his mother's name was Ella, which is so close
to Ellanora, Billie Holiday's birth name ... and so
on with the connections, which brings me

back to the umbilical cord and wondering
why I found myself telling my class about
how thick and dark my son's was and how
it hung on for weeks, no matter how

many times more than the doctor prescribed
I applied alcohol-soaked swabs, sobbing
and full of hope that my son wasn't being
punished because I was too young or
I'd smoked during those first three months …
and I wanted it to fall off … its doing so was my
focus every day … because the doctor said
it was the natural thing, necessary for
healing … for growth. And when it finally did
fall, I sobbed for days, the only physical
proof of our connection now gone out
with the trash.

first summer on Gerald Place

just two weeks past my seventh birthday, too young
to go to Woodstock that year when torrential rain drove
the crowds from the muddy fields of Bethel, shrinking
the Hendrix fans from 400,000 to 40,000,
the same summer we moved into the suburban Cape
Cod my parents would eventually save four times
from foreclosure, the same summer I hugged my favorite uncle's
camouflaged shoulders tight before my mother drove him
off on the first leg of his Vietnam nightmare,
the same summer Neil and the crew proclaimed
one giant step for mankind, the same summer
a Kennedy drove off a bridge and ran, the same
summer Moneta Sleet Jr. won the Pulitzer for
his photograph of Dr. King Jr.'s family, graveside   and
riots in Curacao and Hartford and Stonewall
and others on the streets of Northern Ireland—
all of that and more, and yet what I recall
vividly every time I hear the sound of beating
rain is that hot summer evening,
August 17, 1969, the day my mother turned 24, just
months before being pregnant with her fourth
child after a six-year hiatus from birthing   what I recall
is the beating rain cooling our skin as she invited us
each, by the hand, out of our new home's oppressive heat,
and she ran circles around us, danced barefoot with my father,
encouraged us, laughing, to dance and run circles
too, there on our first patch of grass, sloshing
around on soaking earth, cooling our bodies feet
first, and she taught us there in that rain over Gerald Place
while Hurricane Camille wreaked havoc on the Gulf Coast,
while our nation fought for civil rights and her brother
fought in another tormented wet landscape, the rains that day
were cleansing there on Gerald Place as she taught us
to sing two new songs, become my rainy day forever songs—
"Purple Haze" / / "Give Peace a Chance"

Places She Would Take Me

Uncle John must have seen the look in my eyes because he turned the game down   said I should go to Nonna's room look in her drawers do whatever I wanted. I lifted No. 5 from its dusty place on her gold-rimmed tray   inhaled from the bottle then opened the slim center drawer slid on elbow-length gloves an antique amethyst ring a silk scarf around my shoulders   opened another drawer of photos mass cards matchbooks grocery lists for the A & P near her own tiny office at Day's Travel.   She took her first trip to Kansas City to learn to book and print tickets. She told me places she would take me away from that town where kids didn't come to my block didn't think to be my friend even though I knew the answers and knew too that smart and shy don't go hand in hand because if no one hears you you might as well be dumb. They had more to do than force me out of my shell. Nonna paid attention let me choose one scent then tip bottle to fingertip and we would say *Two for love … two for luck* as we dabbed each temple and behind each ear talking of the places she would take me. Now I light a More Menthol tilt my chin to the ceiling and let out her flirtatious laugh the one that called everyone in the room to her side. Now I open the closet for her mink stole and high heels. I lift a brown box the size of a shoe box but it's heavy like a cinderblock and all taped shut so I take it to Uncle John who drops his drink on the carpet seeing me there looking like her smelling like her holding the box of her ashes.

There on Locust Hill

No matter where in this wide world
I may choose to go, I go knowing
You two are forever planted
There on Locust Hill. How much of you

Is still there, Mother, in your favorite
Blue linen suit, pressed perfectly, perfectly
Accessorized like you might rise up
And walk off to the wedding ceremony

Of one of your grandchildren … events
They experience without you.
Although I am not wed, I wear your ring
Now since Dad removed it on second

Thought just seconds before the final closing
Of the coffin lid. And if remains remain within
Cement slabs, then varnished oak, then satin lining,
Are you still lying by her side, Dad, having forced

Your bony fingers through to hold your one
True love's hand? You are there on Locust Hill,
Names carved in granite, the dates of your lives
Ended abruptly: clover, knot, Claddagh Cross,

One for each. Some days your monument is blanketed
In bird shit and grass clippings; other days the bright
Sun's gleam off the red marble sheen nearly
Blinds me as I still wonder why, all these years later,

Why in the end staying put is what mattered. Other
Days, I wonder why I come to pay tribute
At a place I often wish did not exist outside
The borders of this poem.

Gramatan 5 & 10

1.
Poppy said that First Holy Communion
made a certain mark on me
If I could receive the Body of Christ
I could work the cash register in his
5 & 10 cent store

It was a clunky old thing   thick wooden
drawer   compartments
for each kind of bill   each kind of coin

2.
Be it this day or days later she knows
death is near,

but she chooses not to let her
children, grandchildren know

Instead she makes them laugh

a few breaths from death and chooses not
to let us know what now we know she knew

3.
First I saw the deer
dart toward me from my perch
on the back of the bike

Then I saw the deer
lying close by where I lay,
both of us silent, both of us still

Then I heard the deer
bleating, bleating,
but it was a different deer

It was the mother deer
standing over her fawn
bleating, bleating

I crawled away from the deer,
made the mother deer dash   We left
the fawn   alone silent   alone still

4.
My father in the first pew, all eyes
on him, he casts his eyes   down

He will not see his wife draped
in the white of her new life

He will not see her incensed
for her journey home

He will not see the grieving
touch her casket with fingers   with tears

He raises them only
when the congregation sings

5.
We saw the whales together

spouts first

then sleek and massive humps
still then gleaming baleen plates
The Dolphin Fleet our chapel, its bow our altar,
screeching seagulls, splashing flukes our worship hymns

6.
Poppy said that First Holy Communion
made a certain mark on me

My mother, her father, her mother, my father,
clunky old cash register, silent still fawn,

Gramatan 5 & 10 all long gone,

left me with a sacramental stain

Acknowledgments

Poems in this book, sometimes in earlier versions and with earlier titles, have appeared in the following publications, for which I express grateful acknowledgment to their editors, staff, and sponsors:

"My Son, Philip Seymour Hoffman, and Me" and "No Woman, No Cry"—*5AM*
"splinter" and "Sunday Sauce"—*Paterson Literary Review*
"Locust Hill revisited: December 24, 2003," "it was," and "blue, for Peter"—*The Lake Rises: poems to & for our bodies of water* (Ed. Brandi Katherine Herrera and Lisa Wujnovich, Stockport Flats, 2013)
"nesting," "whittled woman," and "Olive Ridley"—*Adanna Literary Journal*
"Ode to Tomato Soup"—*Tiferet Journal*
"Kemp's ridleys" and "birdsong"—*Jellyfish Whispers*
"Dried-Up Things"—*Digging Through The Fat*
"Places She Would Take Me"—*Pittsburgh Poetry Review*
"Gramatan 5 & 10"—*The Wide Shore*

"My Son, Philip Seymour Hoffman, and Me" was nominated for a Pushcart Prize in 2013 by *5AM*.
"splinter" won Second Prize in the Allen Ginsberg Poetry Awards in 2016, and "Sunday Sauce" was awarded Honorable Mention in 2011.
"Dried-Up Things" won Editor's Choice for 2016 at *Digging Through The Fat*.

Love and Gratitude in Abundance ...

My poems wouldn't be if each of you here hadn't given to me so abundantly ...

It's easy to halve the potato where there's love: Wayne and Tara (you [2] are my sunshine), Kevin, Sierra, Ryan, Grace, Uncle John, Tricia, MaryJo, David, Joann, Michael, Heather, and Laura ... *Ohana! It's five o'clock on a Saturday.* **Without you, nothing.** I love you, each and collectively, madly!

Now you got to be (fresh) to rock with (fresh) (Dougie Fresh) and *If there's something wrong, speak up! (Pete Seeger)*: The Crew ... Peter Kirn (my deep-in-the-well, forever friend), Yesenia Montilla (sister of my heart), Darla Himeles, Mary Brancaccio, Ysabel Gonzalez (soul sisters), Roberto Carlos Garcia, Sosha Pinson, Sean Morrissey, Fletch Fletcher, Brett Haymaker, Lisa Alexander, Cara Armstrong, Heidi Sheridan, Marisa Frasca Patinella ... from those very first days, you have all been my most loyal fans and best critics ... your drive and inspiration, your honesty and generosity, your love and your light are everything.

The moment of change is the only poem (Adrienne Rich): xo, my neighbor ... Laurie Ann Guerrero, my model of true grit!

Art enables us to find ourselves and lose ourselves at the same time (Thomas Merton): close companions on the Drew journey ... and beyond: Jesse Burns, Kathy Engel, Monica Hand, Tamara Hart (<3), Rebecca Gayle Howell, Esther Louise, Chelsea Palermo, Kimberly Rogers, Jane Seitel, Marta Lucia Varga, Lisa Wujnovich, and so on to include every student who contributed their passion and commitment to the most special, unique poetry community that Anne Marie Macari initially envisioned and that we were all so blessed to share in.

In every walk with nature, one receives far more than [s]he seeks (John Muir): My spirits/gurus/advisors/instructors/mentors, thanks for giving me far, far more than I could ever imagine I should seek: Lou Taterka (grade 6), Bev Carboy (grade 12), Joan Larkin (for opening me up), Alicia Ostriker (for taking me back), Anne Marie Macari (my guiding light; our founder, our creator, our heart), Judith Vollmer (for getting me, and for helping me to get me/get it, and for PSH, and so on …).

There are two ways to worry words. One is hoping for the greatest possible beauty in what is created. The other is to tell the truth (June Jordan): My Drew MFA teachers, mentors, and friends … Thanks for the truth … and for joy: Ross Gay, Aracelis Girmay, Joan Larkin, Anne Marie Macari, Jane Mead, Mihaela Moscaliuc, Alicia Ostriker, Patrick Rosal, Ira Sadoff, Judith Vollmer, Michael Waters, Ellen Doré Watson. And Gerald Stern and Jean Valentine, the most loving, wise, and beautiful distinguished poets ever.

Education is the most powerful weapon with which you can change the world (Nelson Mandela): College of Saint Elizabeth English Faculty: for 20+ years of inspiration and motivation … for helping me find me: Kathleen Hunter, Beatrice Kingston, Margaret Roman, Laura Winters.

Only the guy who isn't rowing has time to rock the boat (J-P Sartre): The entire College of Saint Elizabeth Community, past and present, including: Anthony Santamaria, Eileen Specchio, Fr. Tony Ciorra, Kate Brindisi, Kathy Buck, Laura Lee Bowens, Joe Ciccone, Carol Strobeck, Jim Dlugos, Monique Guillory, Helen J. Streubert.

Education is not the filling of a pail, but the lighting of a fire (W.B. Yeats): for my CSE students over all these years … what a gift and privilege it is to share the classroom and other campus spaces together; you who teach me more than I could ever teach you … naming all of you here would make for another whole book, but YES, YOU … You know! IT'S LIT! Thank you.

I have learned that to be with those I like is enough (Walt Whitman): Another book, if I could list the individual names of each of you who has held me up and helped me grow through community … from the Block to the Valley View gang and the St. Bernard's Crowd, especially the Corney and the Long kids, and the Malazinsky, Magliaro, Rich, and A&F Turner families.

Live simply so that all may live (Elizabeth Seton): Sisters of Charity of Saint Elizabeth: S. Alice Lubin, Sister Agnes Vincent Rueshoff, Sister Ellen Joyce, Sister Jean Stabile, Sister Gabriel Mary Donohue, Sister Margaret Mary Conklin, Sister Anne Haarer, Sister Rosemary Moynihan, Sister Jean Hemmer, Sister Julie Scanlon, and so on …

Phenomenal women and phenomenal men … for your models of wisdom, courage, grace, friendship, resilience, and joy: Victor Alcindor, Jane Bourhill, Marina Careirra, Marva Cole Friday, Rich Corney, Melissa Jones Dlugos, Martha Dudich, Joe Farias, Kathleen Gallagher Corney, Joanne Collict Hugues, Pam Linderman, Joe Morris, Carey Salerno, Lisa Sisler, Bruce Smith, Fran Sonneborn, Maureen Underwood, Christine Redmond Waldeyer.

To Liam and Noah and Luke and James for helping me—every Sunday and more—to remember to slooooow down, to be silly, to sing and splash and swing … and for the thrill of adventures on land and at sea! And to your parents and cousins and tanten too.

Again: Roberto Carlos Garcia, publisher extraordinaire; Darla Himeles, exquisite editor; and Raul Villarreal, the man with the vision … and PJK (Aloha!) … and LG (my first teacher of poetry, my forever companion on this poetic journey, "and other poems")… I thank each of you for your belief in and careful attention to me and my poems … MAD LOVE!

My mom was the most genuinely generous person. She taught me by word and deed how necessary, how fulfilling, how beautiful it is to give. My dad joked that if she asked your name, you had made it onto her Christmas list … each one of you mentioned above, in name or thought: you've help me create my own list.

And you, readers … let me know who you are, and I'll joyfully add you to my Christmas (card) list <3

About the Poet

Lynne McEniry was born in Yonkers, NY, and has lived much of her life in northern NJ. Her poems have been published in the *Paterson Literary Review*, *The Lake Rises*, *The Wide Shore*, *Pittsburgh Poetry Review*, and other venues. They have been awarded both Honorable Mention and Second Prize for the Allen Ginsberg Poetry Award and have been nominated for a Pushcart Prize.

Lynne is the associate editor for the recently relaunched *OVS Magazine* and has been a regular guest editor for *Adanna Literary Journal*. She holds an MFA in poetry from Drew University and works at the College of Saint Elizabeth in Morristown, NJ, where she teaches writing and literature and directs the Academic Success Center. This is her first full-length collection of poems. Her website is lynnemceniry.com.

www.ingramcontent.com/pod-product-compliance
Lightning Source LLC
Chambersburg PA
CBHW050544300426
44113CB00012B/2254